HOW TO BE A GOOD COLLEGE ROOMMATE

13-Digit ISBN: 978-1-60433-860-7
10-Digit ISBN: 1-60433-860-1

This book may be ordered by mail from the publisher. Please include $5.99 for postage and handling.
Please support your local bookseller first!

Books published by Cider Mill Press Book Publishers are available at special discounts for bulk
purchases in the United States by corporations, institutions, and other organizations. For more
information, please contact the publisher.

Cider Mill Press Book Publishers
"Where good books are ready for press"
PO Box 454
12 Spring Street
Kennebunkport, Maine 04046
Visit us online!
cidermillpress.com

Typography: Rival, Sackers Gothic
Image Credits: All images used under official license by Shutterstock.com.

Printed in China
2 3 4 5 6 7 8 9 0

HOW TO
BE A GOOD
COLLEGE
ROOMMATE

RODGER HOLST

CIDER MILL
PRESS

BOOK
PUBLISHERS
KENNEBUNKPORT, MAINE

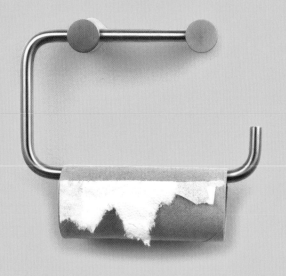

DON'T BE AN ASSH*LE.

DON'T BE AN ASSH*LE.

DON'T BE AN ASSH*LE.

DON'T BE AN ASSH*LE.

DON'T BE AN ASSH*LE.

DON'T BE AN ASSH*LE.

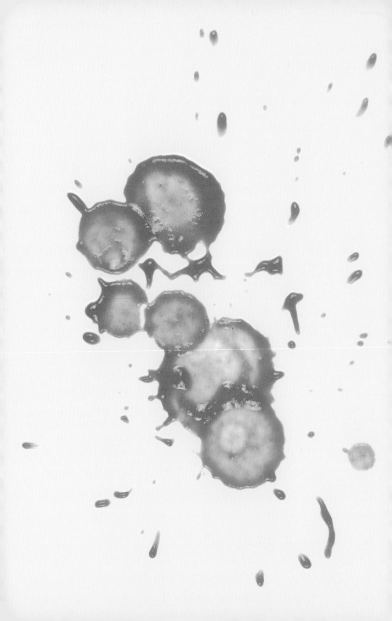

DON'T BE AN ASSH*LE.

DON'T BE AN ASSH*LE.

DON'T BE AN ASSH*LE.

DON'T BE AN ASSH*LE.

FINAL REPORT

DON'T BE AN ASSH*LE.

DON'T BE AN ASSH*LE.

DON'T BE AN ASSH*LE.

DON'T BE AN ASSH*LE.

DON'T BE AN ASSH*LE.

DON'T BE AN ASSH*LE.

DON'T BE AN ASSH*LE.

ween es lo

ses

paid

159.67
157.69
5.18
5.87
5.4
70
(01

Bas
the a

30 days
If we
State
and

DON'T BE AN ASSH*LE.

DON'T BE AN ASSH*LE.

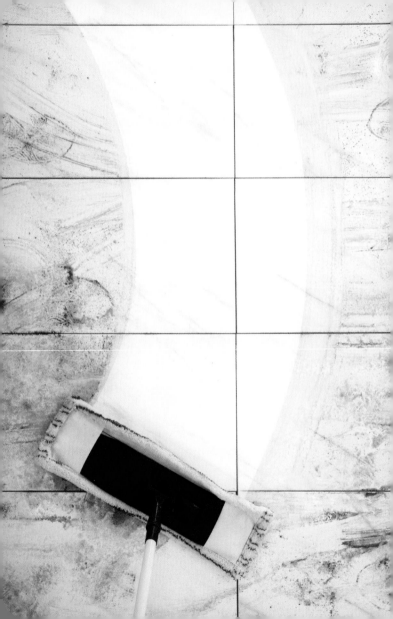

DON'T BE AN ASSH*LE.

DON'T BE AN ASSH*LE.

DON'T BE AN ASSH*LE.

DON'T BE AN ASSH*LE.

DON'T BE AN ASSH*LE.

DON'T BE AN ASSH*LE.

DON'T BE AN ASSH*LE.

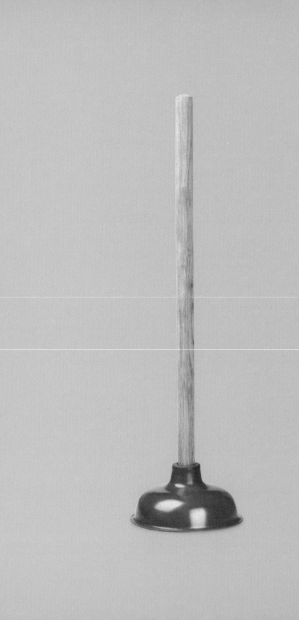

DON'T BE AN ASSH*LE.

DON'T BE AN ASSH*LE.

DON'T BE AN ASSH*LE.

DON'T BE AN ASSH*LE.

About the Author

Rodger Holst was such a terrible roommate that the board of trustees at his college eventually exiled him to a tent deep in the woods. He made the most of this time alone, and has gathered those epiphanies here to keep others from encountering a similar fate.

About Cider Mill Press Book Publishers

Good ideas ripen with time. From seed to harvest, Cider Mill Press brings fine reading, information, and entertainment together between the covers of its creatively crafted books. Our Cider Mill bears fruit twice a year, publishing a new crop of titles each spring and fall.

"Where Good Books Are Ready for Press"

Visit us online at
cidermillpress.com
or write to us at
PO Box 454
12 Spring St.
Kennebunkport, Maine 04046